Dear Parent:
Your child's love of reading starts here!

Every child learns to read in a different way and at his or her own speed. Some go back and forth between reading levels and read favorite books again and again. Others read through each level in order. You can help your young reader improve and become more confident by encouraging his or her own interests and abilities. From books your child reads with you to the first books he or she reads alone, there are I Can Read Books for every stage of reading:

SHARED READING
Basic language, word repetition, and whimsical illustrations, ideal for sharing with your emergent reader

1 BEGINNING READING
Short sentences, familiar words, and simple concepts for children eager to read on their own

2 READING WITH HELP
Engaging stories, longer sentences, and language play for developing readers

3 READING ALONE
Complex plots, challenging vocabulary, and high-interest topics for the independent reader

4 ADVANCED READING
Short paragraphs, chapters, and exciting themes for the perfect bridge to chapter books

I Can Read Books have introduced children to the joy of reading since 1957. Featuring award-winning authors and illustrators and a fabulous cast of beloved characters, I Can Read Books set the standard for beginning readers.

A lifetime of discovery begins with the magical words **"I Can Read!"**

Visit www.icanread.com for information
on enriching your child's reading experience.

I Can Read!

BEGINNING
1
READING

Pinkalicious
and the Babysitter

For Jessica

—V.K.

The author gratefully acknowledges
the artistic and editorial contributions of
Daniel Griffo and Natalie Engel.

I Can Read Book® is a trademark of HarperCollins Publishers.

Pinkalicious and the Babysitter
Copyright © 2017 by Victoria Kann

PINKALICIOUS and all related logos and characters are trademarks of Victoria Kann. Used with permission.

Based on the HarperCollins book *Pinkalicious* written by
Victoria Kann and Elizabeth Kann, illustrated by Victoria Kann
All rights reserved. Manufactured in China.
No part of this book may be used or reproduced in any manner whatsoever without
written permission except in the case of brief quotations embodied in critical articles and reviews.
For information address HarperCollins Children's Books, a division of HarperCollins Publishers,
195 Broadway, New York, NY 10007.
www.icanread.com

Library of Congress Control Number: 2016957938

ISBN 978-0-06-256689-8 (trade bdg.) — ISBN 978-0-06-256688-1 (pbk.)

17 18 19 20 21 SCP 10 9 8 7 6 5 4 3 2 1
❖
First Edition

I Can Read!

BEGINNING READING 1

Pinkalicious
and the Babysitter

by Victoria Kann

HARPER
An Imprint of HarperCollinsPublishers

It was a big day at our house.

Mommy and Daddy were going out.

Peter and I were staying home

with our babysitter, Maya.

"Do you have to go?"

Peter asked Mommy and Daddy.

"Yes," Daddy said.

"But we'll be back," said Mommy.

Peter looked anxious.

"It's okay, Peter," I said.

"You were too little to remember,

but Maya is lots of fun!

She loves to play games.

Sometimes she even

makes hot chocolate."

"Hot chocolate? Yum!" said Peter.

After Maya arrived

we gave Mommy and Daddy

good-bye hugs.

Peter squeezed them extra-tight.

I could tell he was still worried.

"What can we play?"

I asked Maya.

"Hide-and-Go-Pink? Pinkopoly?"

"How about Roll the Pink Dice?"

said Maya.

"I'll show you how to play."

Maya drew rows of squares

on a big piece of paper.

She placed some dice on the table.

"Pinkalicious, you go first,"

she said.

I rolled a five.

"Move five spaces while
balancing on one leg
like a pink flamingo!" said Maya.
Peter and I giggled.

Next it was Peter's turn.

He rolled a two.

"You can move two squares

after you do two somersaults!"

Maya said.

Peter tucked his head and rolled
and rolled—
right onto his stuffed bear!
It was too funny.

"Now it's my turn," said Maya.

She tossed the dice.

"Six," she said. "What's my task?"

Peter and I looked at each other.

"Meow like a kitten," said Peter.

"While twirling," I said.

"And sing *Old PinkDonald*!"

"Oh my," said Maya.

She twirled and meowed, then sang.

We all fell over laughing!

17

Soon it was time for lunch.

"What are we having?" asked Peter.

"Peas and fish sticks," said Maya.

Peter and I made yucky faces.

"No peas if you please," I said.

"Let's play a new game," said Maya.
"This one's called Eat Your P's.
Every time you say a word
with the letter P in it,
you have to take a bite."

"I've never played

this before," I said.

"You said *played*!"

Maya said, laughing.

"Take a bite."

"Oops," I said, then ate a spoonful.

"Your turn, Peter," I said.

"You said *Peter*!

That starts with *P*!" he said.

I took another bite!

This game was hard!

Our peas were gone in no time.

Maya made us hot chocolate

as a treat for clearing our plates.

She even added pink marshmallows!

I got to use Mommy's favorite mug.

I had painted it for her in art class.

"Refills?" asked Maya.

"Yay!" Peter cheered.

"But I want Mommy's mug this time!"
Peter tried to take the mug from me,
but it slipped.

"Uh-oh!" Peter gasped.

The mug fell to the ground and broke.

"Mommy's mug!" Peter said.

He started to cry.

Maya picked up the broken pieces.

"Accidents happen," she said.

"Your mom will understand."

Peter cried harder.

I looked at the broken pieces.

They were still very pretty.

"It's okay.

I have an idea!" I said.

"We'll make a mosaic!" I said.

"I learned how to make them in art class."

Peter stopped crying.

"What's a moo-say-ick?" he asked.

"I'll show you!" I said.

I grabbed some glue and cardboard.

We arranged the broken pieces.

"Be careful of the sharp edges," I said.

"Just in time!

Your parents are home," said Maya.

"What's this?" Mommy asked.

"I'm sorry. I broke your mug,"

Peter said,

"but we turned it into art!"

"I love it," Mommy said.

"It's art with heart!" said Daddy.

"A big heart," I said proudly.

Mommy gave me a hug.

"Just like yours," she said.